Contents

KT-417-959

Cars inside out

A car is a very complicated machine. Inside a car there are thousands of parts, from large metal sheets in the body to tiny electronic components that control the engine. In this book, diagrams show you all the main parts of a car. Here you can see the inside and outside of a Nissan Acura NSX sports car, with details of its main parts.

Electrics

A car has hundreds of electrical parts. These include lights, motors that move the wipers and windows, locks and displays.

Wheels

The wheels let the car roll along the road. The tyres grip the road and help to give the passengers a smooth ride.

Left-hand and right-hand

For the United Kingdom and some other countries, such as Australia, cars are built with the steering wheel on the right-hand side of the car, as in this sports car. For most countries, the steering wheel is on the left. Most other car parts are in the same place.

Cars

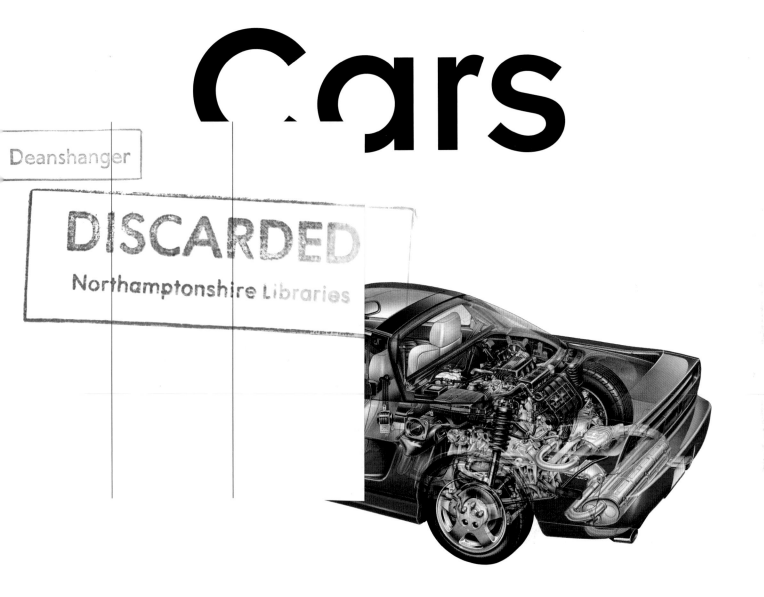

Chris Oxlade

WAYLAND

First published in 2008 by Wayland

Copyright © Wayland 2008

Wayland
Hachette Children's Books
338 Euston Road
London NW1 3BH

Wayland Australia
Level 17/207 Kent Street
Sydney, NSW 2000

Senior Editor: Jennifer Schofield

Produced by Tall Tree Ltd
Editor: Rob Scott Colson
Designer: Darren Jordan
Consultant: Ben Russell

British Library Cataloguing in Publication Data
Oxlade, Chris,
  Cars. - (Machines inside out)
    1. Automobiles - Juvenile literature
    I. Title
    629.2'22

ISBN 978-0-7502-5322-2

Printed in China

Wayland is a division of Hachette Children's Books, an Hachette Livre UK company.

Acknowledgements
Cover John Prescott/istockphoto, Kevin Hulsey Illustration, Inc.
6t Kevin Hulsey Illustration, Inc., 6b Markwr/Dreamstime.com,
7 Kevin Hulsey Illustration, Inc., 8 Steve Mann/Dreamstime.com,
9t Gary Beet/Dreamstime.com, 9b Kaikai/Dreamstime.com,
10 Ryan Jorgensen/Dreamstime.com, 11t Kevin Hulsey Illustration, Inc., 11b Kirsty Pargeter/Dreamstime.com,
12l Zoediak/Dreamstime.com, 12r Kevin Hulsey Illustration, Inc.,13 Stephen Sweet/Dreamstime.com,
14–15 Dannyphoto80/Dreamstime.com, 15 Stephen Sweet/Dreamstime.com, 16b NASA, 16t Kevin Hulsey Illustration, Inc., 17t Ahanix, 17b Kevin Hulsey Illustration, Inc.,18 Kevin Hulsey Illustration, Inc., 19t Bogdan Lazar/Dreamstime.com, 19bl Kevin Hulsey Illustration, Inc., 19br Nancy Thiele/Dreamstime.com, 20l Felix Alim/istockphoto, 20r Yang Yu/Dreamstime.com, 21 Stephen Sweet/istockphoto, 22–23 Kevin Hulsey Illustration, Inc., 22 Saltov/Dreamstime.com, 23 Eric Wong/Dreamstime.com, 24–25 Tim Wright/CORBIS, 25 Jorge Delgado/istockphoto, 26 Kevin Hulsey Illustration, Inc., 27t Roberto Marinello/ Dreamstime.com, 27b NASA

Note to parents and teachers
The website addresses (URLs) included in this book were valid at the time of going to press. However, because of the nature of the Internet, it is possible that some addresses may have changed, or sites may have changed or closed down since publication. While the author and Publisher regret any inconvenience this may cause the readers, no responsibility for any such changes can be accepted by either the author or the Publisher.

Engine

The engine drives the car along by turning the wheels. The fuel system and exhaust are both attached to the engine.

Suspension

The suspension lets the wheels move up and down as the car goes over bumps. It keeps the tyres touching the road.

Bodywork

The bodywork is part of the strong shell of the car. It supports the other parts, makes the car aerodynamic and protects passengers.

Car structure

The main part of a car is its body shell. It is made of flat pieces, called panels, and long, thin pieces, called pillars and struts. These parts are normally made from steel. Sports cars often have an aluminium body shell because aluminium is lighter than steel, so the car can go faster. Together, the sheets and struts make a strong structure, like a box.

Building a body shell

The parts of a body shell are made by machines called presses. A press bends a flat sheet of steel into a curved body panel or strut. The different parts are joined together in a car factory by welding and gluing. The doors, bonnet and boot are added later.

Space frames

Some sports cars have a structure called a space frame instead of a body shell. This sort of frame is made up of tubes welded together to make a strong three-dimensional structure. The frame is then covered with thin body panels.

Painting the shell

The shell is sprayed with anti-corrosion chemicals. This stops water getting to it and making it go rusty. The shell is then sprayed with layers of paint.

Roof pillar

Body panel

Connections for rear suspension

Floor panel

Wheels

Wheels are attached to the car by bearings, which let them spin freely. At least two of the wheels are turned by the engine. Tyres grip the road so that the car can turn corners, speed up and slow down. Suspension allows the wheels to move up and down on bumps. It keeps the tyres in contact with the road, and keeps the driver and passengers as comfortable as possible.

Tyres and treads

Tyres are made from rubber strengthened inside by thin layers of steel. This makes them strong but flexible. They are filled with air. The grooves on the outside of a tyre are called the tread. In the wet, the tread pushes water away, letting the tyre grip the road.

Shocks and springs

On the opposite page is the suspension of a sports car. A suspension arm connects the wheel to the car, but lets it move up and down. Each wheel also has a spring and shock absorber, which together support the car.

TECH FACT

Some cars have active suspension. This means that an electronic system controls the suspension on each wheel. When the car goes around a corner, the system adjusts the height of the suspension on each wheel so that the car stays level. Active suspension helps to stop a car from skidding.

Independent suspension

Most modern family cars have independent suspension. This means that each wheel has its own spring and shock absorber. The absorber is not connected to the other wheels, so if one wheel goes over a bump, the other wheels are not affected.

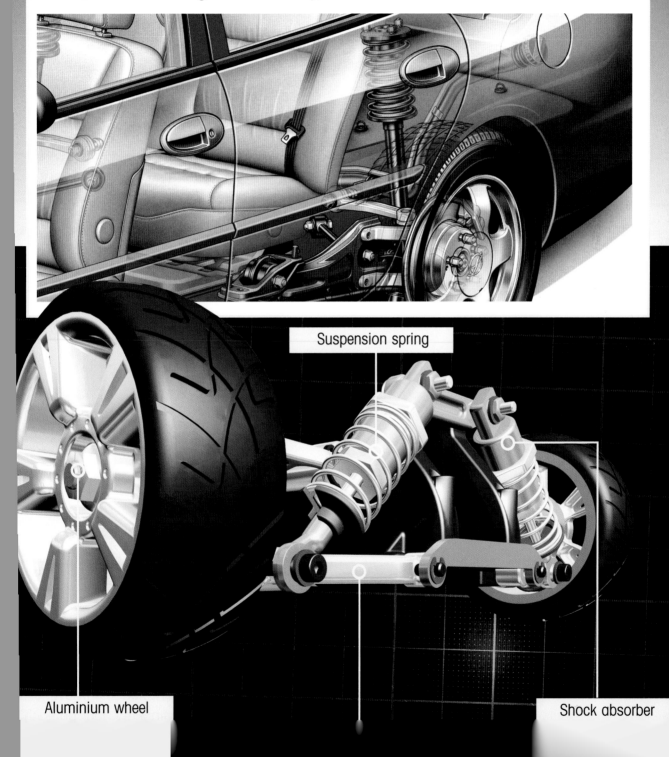

Suspension spring

Aluminium wheel

Shock absorber

Cylinders and pistons

The engine is a machine that turns the car's wheels. Cylinders are spaces inside the engine, about the shape and size of tin cans. Fuel combusts, or burns, inside the cylinders. This is why car engines are called internal combustion engines. Pistons slide up and down the cylinders. When fuel burns, it pushes the pistons down. The pistons turn a crankshaft, which is connected to the wheels.

Turning the crankshaft

Each piston has a connecting rod. When a piston is pushed by the explosion of fuel in a cylinder, the connecting rod pushes the crankshaft round. The engine opposite is called an in-line four (or straight four) because its four cylinders are arranged in a line.

Lubricating the engine

Inside an engine, metal parts are constantly moving against each other. For example, the pistons move inside the cylinders. Engine oil lets them move without rubbing. The oil is pumped around by an oil pump, and kept clean by oil filters like these here.

Engine arrangements

The in-line four engine is the most common type of engine. But there are other arrangements. The engine above is a V-8. It has eight cylinders – four on each side. The two sets of four cylinders are arranged in a 'V' shape. A V-8 engine is much more powerful than an in-line four.

Cylinder

Crankshaft

Connecting rod

The four-stroke cycle

As an engine works, each cylinder follows a sequence of moves called the four-stroke cycle. A valve lets in a fuel and air mixture, which is ignited electrically by a spark plug and drives the piston down the cylinder. A valve lets out the exhaust gases after the mixture has burned.

The four strokes
The first stroke is the intake stroke, when fuel and air are sucked into the cylinder. The compression stroke squeezes the mixture. Then, after the power stroke, exhaust gases are pushed out in the final stroke.

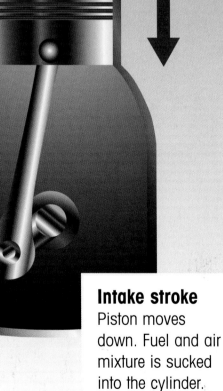

Intake stroke
Piston moves down. Fuel and air mixture is sucked into the cylinder.

Compression stroke
Piston moves up. Fuel and air are squeezed into the top of the cylinder.

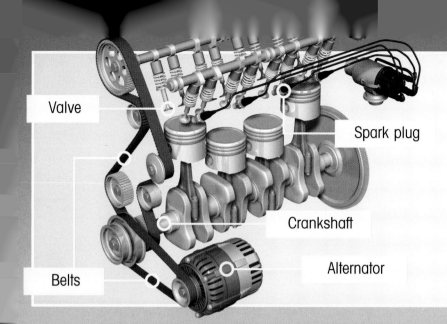

Valve

Spark plug

Crankshaft

Belts

Alternator

Controlling the timing

The engine's valves must open and close at the right time, and the spark plugs must spark at the right moment. The valves are opened and closed by camshafts, which are turned by a belt from the crankshaft. The spark plugs work electronically. Another belt turns the alternator to make electricity for the spark plugs.

Power stroke
Fuel burns.
Piston is pushed down.

Exhaust stroke
Piston moves up.
Exhaust gases are pushed out.

Fuel and exhaust

A car engine needs fuel to work. It is stored in the fuel tank and burns in the cylinders. The fuel system moves the fuel from the tank to the cylinders. It also supplies air to the cylinders. The fuel needs air so that it can burn. After the fuel burns, waste gases are left over and the exhaust system removes these waste gases from the engine.

The fuel system

The fuel is moved along pipes called fuel lines by the fuel pump. Air is sucked into the engine through an air filter that removes dirt from it. Then fuel is sprayed into it and it goes into the cylinders. The accelerator pedal controls how much air and fuel go into the cylinders.

Accelerator pedal

Turbocharging

Sports cars and larger touring cars often have a device called a turbocharger (often called a 'turbo'). The turbo pumps air into the engine, which allows more fuel to be burned in the cylinders. The turbo is powered by exhaust gases.

Catalytic converter

The exhaust system carries exhaust gases to the back of the car, where they are released into the air. The catalytic converter contains special chemicals (called catalysts) that change harmful gases into less harmful gases.

Filler cap

Fuel line

Exhaust pipe

Cooling the engine

An engine gets hot when it is working. The heat comes from the burning fuel and from the engine parts rubbing together. The engine must be cooled, or it will become too hot and stop working. Heat is removed from the engine by a car's cooling system. Most cars have a liquid-cooled engine, where water carries away the heat.

Hot and cold

Cool water flows into the engine and through spaces inside the engine block. Heat from the engine is transferred into the water, making the engine cooler and the water hotter. The hot water flows to the radiator, where it is cooled.

Radiator

CALIFORNIA
20150 A

Cooling with a fan

The radiator is at the front of the car. When the car is moving, air flows over the radiator, cooling the water inside. When the car is still with the engine running, a fan blows air over the radiator.

Radiator fins

The radiator has thousands of thin metal fins. This gives it a very large surface area, so heat from the water inside is transferred into the air.

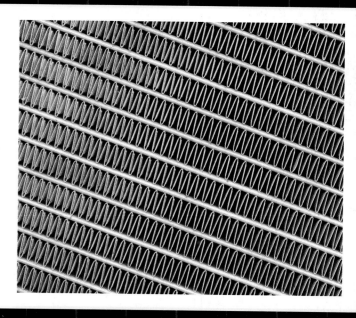

Transsmission

A car's transmission connects the engine to the wheels. It is made up of the clutch, the gearbox and drive shafts. These parts allow the driver to stop, start and control the car's speed. The clutch lets the driver disconnect the gearbox and wheels from the engine. The driver uses the clutch before changing from one gear to another.

Automatic gears

Cars can be fitted with an automatic transmission. This changes gears by itself as the car speeds up and slows down.

The gearbox

The gearbox allows the engine to turn the wheels at different speeds. The box is full of cogs of different sizes. Moving the gear lever makes different cogs interlock. Each combination of cogs is called a gear. Low gears are used for starting the car and slow speeds. High gears are used for fast driving.

Shaft to wheels

Universal joints

Spinning rods, called drive shafts, connect the gearbox to the wheels. They have joints in them called universal joints. These joints allow drive shafts to bend around corners. They also let the shafts drive wheels even when they are bumping up and down.

Shaft from clutch

Gear cog

Secondary sh

Steering and brakes

A driver controls a car using the steering wheel, foot pedals and the gear lever. The steering wheel makes the front wheels turn from side to side. Two foot pedals control the clutch (see page 20) and the accelerator (see page 16). Another pedal controls the brakes. The brakes slow the car by stopping the wheels turning. Cars with automatic transmission do not have a clutch pedal.

Steering connections

The simplest steering system is called rack and pinion steering. Here, a cog, called the pinion, on the bottom of the steering column makes a rod, called the rack, move from side to side. The two ends of the rack twist the wheels to steer the car.

Power steering

Most cars have power assisted steering, where the car helps the driver to steer the car. A pump powered by the engine pumps hydraulic fluid, which moves the steering rack. The flow of fluid is controlled by the steering column.

Brake discs and pads

Each wheel has a metal brake disc attached to it. When the driver presses the brake pedal, two pads squeeze the disc, which slows the wheel.

Brake pipe

Safety and comfort

There are many parts inside a modern car that are designed to make it comfortable for drivers and passengers, and as safe as possible should an accident happen. Comfort features include heating, air conditioning, electric seats and music and video systems. Safety features include crumple zones, seat belts, air bags and anti-lock brakes (see page 23).

Crumple zones

The body shell of a car contains sections known as crumple zones. These are designed to collapse and absorb the energy of a collision. There are crumple zones at the front and back of a car. Some cars also have side-impact bars inside the doors.

Seatbelts and airbags

A seatbelt holds your in your seat during an accident. It stops you flying forwards and being hurt. Small children sit in booster seats so that the seatbelt fits them properly. In an accident, an airbag inflates (blows up), and stops the driver hitting the dashboard.

TECH FACT

All makes and models of cars are tested to see what will happen to them in a collision. These tests are called impact tests or crash tests. Dummies inside the cars show what would happen to a person inside. The results of impact tests let people see which are the safest makes of car.

Electric cars

An electric car has an electric motor instead of a petrol or diesel engine. The electricity to turn the motor comes from batteries inside the car, or from a fuel cell. Electric cars do not burn fuel directly, so they do not produce exhaust fumes. However, their batteries need to be recharged regularly.

Battery power

The motor in an electric car must be very powerful to move the car. This means that it needs a lot of electricity. The electricity comes from a number of large batteries under the floor or in the boot. The batteries are the heaviest part of the car.

Electric motor

Electronic controls

12-volt batteries

Recharging

When the batteries in an electric car run out of electricity, they need to be recharged. The car is plugged into the mains electricity. After a few hours of charging, the batteries are full and the car can go again.

Fuel cell cars

A fuel cell is a bit like a battery. It makes electricity from chemicals that are pumped into it. This electric car has a fuel cell that works its motor. The cell uses a chemical called hydrogen. NASA uses fuel cells to launch space shuttles.

TECH FACT

A hybrid car is a car that is powered by both a petrol engine and an electric motor. Energy produced when the car brakes is used to charge the batteries and is mostly used to power the car when driving in cities. This makes the car more energy efficient than normal cars since it uses less fuel.

Glossary

Accelerate
To speed up.

Alternator
A device that turns movement into electricity.

Bearing
Part of a car that holds a wheel in place but lets it spin round easily.

Body shell
The main part of a car. It gives the car its strength and supports all the other parts.

Carbon-fibre reinforced plastic
A composite material made by embedding thin carbon fibres in hard plastic.

Component
An object that is part of a larger, more complex machine.

Cylinder
A space inside an engine where fuel burns.

Exhaust
The parts of a car that carry waste gases away from the engine.

Filter
A device that removes pieces of dirt from a liquid or a gas.

Fuel system
The parts of a car that store fuel and pump it to the engine's cylinders.

Hydraulic
Describes a machine that has parts moved by liquid pumped along pipes.

Piston
Part of an engine that slides up and down a cylinder.

Sensor
A device that detects things, such as whether a car door is closed, or engine temperature.

Shock absorber
Part of a suspension that stops the suspension spring getting too squashed or stretched.

Skid
When a car slides along the road without one or more of the wheels turning. It happens when the tyres lose their grip on the road.

Suspension
Part of a car that lets the wheels move up and down as the car goes over bumps.

Suspension unit
Part of a car suspension, made up of a spring and a shock absorber.

Valve
Part of an engine that opens temporarily to let fuel into a cylinder or exhaust gases out of a cylinder.

Welding
A way of joining two pieces of metal together by heating them up and pressing them together.

Further reading

Top Trumps Ultimate Cars
Matt Saunders (JH Haynes, 2006)

Top Trumps Extreme Wheels
Tim Oldham (JH Haynes, 2006)

DK Eyewitness Car
Richard Sutton
(Dorling Kindersley, 2005)

The Encyclopedia of Classic Cars
Martin Buckley (Southwater, 2003)

Useful websites

auto.howstuffworks.com/engine.html
A guide to how car engines work.

www.bbc.co.uk/topgear
The website of the TV show Top Gear.

auto.howstuffworks.com/ transmission3.html
Animation of a four-speed gearbox.

www.bmw-werk-muenchen.de/ lowband/com/en/index.html
Virtual tour of BMW's car plant in Munich, Germany, showing how their cars are made.

Index